Dear Chr
With P,
Why bother with the old man
Selling water by the river
Why? You wonder.
Love. Jac/2010.

Meditation

A Primer
For The Primate

BY ZAC TIANNE

In ancient times of crisis
Those who meditated well did not think
Those who thought well did not fret
Those who fretted well did not agonize
Those who agonized well did not despair
Those who despaired well did not lose their mind
To the Medicine Men.

ZT 2010
(Inspired by Zhuge Liang
Warrior and Administrator—died 233 AD
My Teacher from the grave.)

Meditation is a brain tranquilizer. The brain is used by
the mind to bolster the ego. Tranquilize it and the mind
has less to work with. In Creole, 'trankil' means quiet,
peaceful, still, silent, alone.

ZT 2010
(Inspired by Père Margeot
Cardinal—died 2009 AD

My best friend
My worst enemy
My imagination

Contents

Introduction   9

Chapter One
    That Was Zen, This Is How   13
    I Think, Therefore I Hurt   13
    Still Your Body, Still Your Mind   15
    Take It Lying Down   17
    A Bum Deal   21
    Get Physical   25
    Now Work Those Muscles   27
    Ready, Set, Breathe   32
    Sitting Pretty   35
    Take A Ride   39
    Catch Your Breath   41
    Go Mental   42
    Drawing a Blank   44
    The Trip Home   45
    The Secret Of My Failure   47
    Other Incidental Factors   50
    The End Is Near   54
    That Empty Feeling   54
    Running On Empty   55

Chapter Two
    Your Journey   63

Appendix A
    Mental States That Would Drive Sane
    and Insane People To Meditate   67
Appendix B
    I Hurt, Therefore I Rant   73

Introduction

With a calm and clear mind you can be more productive at work and more relaxed when you're playing. And the odds are good that you'd be more resilient to stress and enjoy better physical health through better mental health. The way to get a calm mind is to render it still for a while on a regular basis and to set it free. By a still mind, I don't mean an idle mind but one that is clear of any thoughts or reflection. And by free, I mean free from dependency on pleasant thoughts, memories, a good book or movie, a sound, a word, music or a holy verse. And your free mind is in that state of stillness while you are wide awake. There is a way to meditate that can take your mind there in a simple and efficient manner.

I used and will continue to use the term 'meditate' because it conveys the message in terms that are commonly understood, but actually what I'll be getting you to do to achieve that mental stillness is a physical workout rather than a mental activity. In fact, mental activity is what you want to avoid; it's the last thing you want when what you're trying to do is to give the mind a break.

Most of us must learn to meditate from books because the luxury of personal instructions from a teacher at a secluded temple up in the mountains is usually not an option. Besides, the drive to work alone would kill you.

The good news is there are many books on the subject. The bad news is most of them take 15 to 20 chapters, or 300 to 400 pages to teach, explain, justify, glorify and often mystify it when the instructions for learning to meditate successfully need only take up one chapter, or about 30 to 40 pages. Besides being just too much information (even if most of it is good information) for a newbie, much of what is discussed on those pages is mostly incomprehensible to someone who is not already proficient in meditation. I don't doubt that you understand what the words mean but it's unlikely that you truly understand what they are describing. You need to actually experience what is being described to really understand what they're writing about. It's like explaining how delicious the cuisines of the civilized world are to Tarzan on his first day out of the jungle. He has to eat the food to begin to understand you.

So here is a solution to this problem. Besides showing you a most effective method of meditation, I've also done it in one chapter. This is a primer on meditation. It contains the instructions you need to learn to meditate successfully. The instructions involve nothing esoteric or difficult to understand. They require you to do two things that you already know how to do—you just need to do them in a certain way. I want to get you to that still mind, where it all begins, using the shortest route possible. You can then go back to those books if you still need a quick intellectual or mystic fix—you still have that choice. I have personally used this method to enjoy a still mind and I hope you can too.

The two things you need to do in order to meditate successfully are:

- sit still;
- work out.

And you're doing this while keeping your entire being absolutely still. This primer gives detailed instructions on how to sit still and what exercises to perform.

The other good thing about this primer being only as long as the average chapter in most books is that you can finish reading it in a few hours. You can then study it for the rest of your life as you learn to meditate, write your own version, or at least your own chapter, and log your personal journey. That's why there is even a Chapter Two.

Appendices A and B are not instructions and can be overlooked altogether.

Appendix A lists examples of mental states that would drive any sane or insane person to seek help from meditation. Some of them are bound to sound familiar to you and are probably the reason you're even reading this primer.

Appendix B is just an old man ranting and raving about man, religion, society, love, hate, politics—you know— life. They are thoughts and opinions that are relevant to me personally but are totally unnecessary for you to learn how to meditate successfully. So you'll be none the worse if you just ignore them. But I hope I get to hear yours some day in Chapter Two.

Writing this primer was initially to document my discoveries because I thought it was important for my kids to take advantage of what I learned, and not just what I earned. But then I thought if others can benefit from it (just the learning, that is) then it may be worth making it available to one and all.

CHAPTER ONE
(And Only)

That Was Zen, This Is How

The meditation techniques I'm proposing in this primer are based on practices that are also found in Zen, Chi Kung, Tai Chi, Yoga, Catholicism and sports generally. But under my approach, it's preferable to steer clear of philosophy, deep thinking, the search for the meaning of life, our existence on Earth, our place in the Universe, experiencing pure existence, being or reaching out to a higher power somewhere up there or down there. It's not that I want you to abandon these intellectual or religious quests, but to learn to meditate using my method and make your mind still, they will get in the way. They make the mind busy when what I want to teach you is to clear your mind of everything and hopefully get a break from the trials and tribulations of daily living.

This primer therefore focuses simply on HOW to meditate; what to do, what seems to work most easily, what produces the best results based on my own training and experience in its practice.

I Think, Therefore I Hurt

With man's highly developed brain came the mind, the marvel that lets him almost control the elements, cure diseases, change his appearance, produce delicious nutrition, fly with birds, dive with fish and travel in space with aliens. The price he pays for these 'un-animal' advantages are self-adoration, self-pity, self-loathing, superstitions, dirty politics, social posturing, religious hierarchy, Heaven, Hell, imaginary superheroes like angels, demons, spirits, ghosts, saints and gods. The taxes he pays on top of that price are the elaborate structures, rites and rituals he created to materialize these mental lapses for those who need to see and touch, leading to a sense of superiority for the leaders, of inferiority for the followers, and of inclusion and exclusion, and just a lot of confusion for those not yet exposed to their machinations. His ability to use symbols to describe incredible images, tell tall tales and piece together awesome sounds further bolsters these inventions leading the masses that follow him after his body has returned to dust to recite the mumbo jumbo according to John, Paul, George and Ringo or to chase the sound of one hand clapping instead of simply enjoying the music or the sound of silence.

Meditation, in its popular form, comes with a price tag derived from the same value scheme. That's why there is so much literature on the subject. What's happened to it is the same thing that has plagued and burdened the simple, precious teachings of great men like Confucius the dedicated scholar, Gautama the compassionate prince, Sun Tzu the visionary warlord, Jesus the enlightened carpenter, Zhuge Liang the wise warrior and Muhammad the ethical merchant. The Medicine Men came. The Medicine Men cometh still.

The meditation technique I've picked up over the years can discharge those heavy debts that most of us have inherited from the Medicine Men through generations via traditions and social norms. But before we discuss actual technique, let me cover some basic characteristics of mental activity that made it possible for us to run up so much debt under that value system and how, by controlling these characteristics through meditation, it's possible to offload those debts.

Still Your Body, Still Your Mind

Mental activity results from stimulus that is both external and internal to the brain. External stimulus is transmitted to the brain via our sensory organs as well as from our entire body via nerve endings. Internal stimulus is generated within the brain when you reflect upon the external stimulus supplied to the brain, upon further internal stimulus generated as a result of such reflection or original internal stimulus initiated within the brain at will or at random. Here are some examples. External: You witness a traffic accident; internal: You wonder if the people in the vehicles are hurt. External: You hear a moving account of Jesus' trek to his own crucifixion; internal: You resolve to treat your fellow men with more compassion. Internal: You suddenly remember that you were supposed to get some cash at the ATM; internal: You think what an idiot you are. A more general example of internal stimulus generated and nurtured within the brain at will and at random is how your imagination works. In a nutshell, most people's minds never stop receiving and creating stimulus and are always active during their waking hours.

Meditation is about controlling the stimulus to the brain, thereby controlling mental activity. Controlling external stimulus is not difficult but it's not always easy either. Controlling internal stimulus is not difficult, it's nigh impossible. Luckily for us, it can be done with relative ease when the body is enlisted to help out.

When you're totally engrossed in solving a problem, the internal-to-external stimulus ratio is probably in the 90-to-10 range (the 10 is for when your nose is itchy.) When you're watching a movie or a football game, unless it's painfully slow and boring or your team is trailing by 28 points, the ratio is likely to be 50-to-50. When you're working out, running or just taking a walk it's probably closer to the 20-to-80 range. When you meditate, the process is aimed at achieving a ratio of 10-to-90, and ultimately leading to a ratio of 0-to-0.

Now, we've discussed ratio but there is also the level or volume of that mental activity that is pertinent. In solving the problem, it's high; when watching the movie or the game, it's likely not as high, but hopefully still high due to excitement or amusement. When exercising, running, it's probably medium to low, unless that dog is chasing you again. In meditation, it's low, very low. In fact, when you are meditating successfully, the volume should be at practically zero.

You don't need me to tell you that this is not a scientific explanation of how the brain works. What it is though is a broad brush characterization of mental activity that serves the purpose of explaining the need to control stimuli to the brain in order to bring stillness to it. It will help show what happens when you're meditating and why you would even bother to do it. What I illustrated is what I have observed, especially the ratios and hopefully it will help you understand what it is we're trying to achieve by meditating.

But enough of all this discussion already that is causing so much thinking. Let me get down to tangibles and specifics. To meditate successfully, you minimize the external stimulus by going somewhere quiet and by keeping your body absolutely still. You then minimize the internal stimulus by reducing your activities to a simple physical exercise and then use that same exercise to engage the mind. That's how you ensure that minimal stimulus is being generated within the brain. So find a quiet room and let's get going.

Take It Lying Down

With all this in mind—no reverse pun intended—let's try a few things. First, try lying down in bed and not moving. If you fall asleep, that's called sleeping, not meditating. See, you have to keep your body as still as possible but you also have to remain wide awake.

Let's try the next thing and start the easy way. Lie on the floor, flat on your back, knees raised, pointing toward the ceiling or legs straight parallel to the floor, your arms at a naturally comfortable angle and distance from your sides. Your hands should be relaxed, whether palms up, palms down, or resting on their side. With knees raised, if your feet are dry you may find that they will slip away from you, so wear some socks to give them some grip. This is quite a comfortable position and it's relaxing. So stay like that for a while and don't move at all.

When you're relaxed, try not to think of anything. That may work for a little while but soon enough, thoughts flood the mind. So as an alternative mental activity for the brain so it's not racing around trying to remember if you left something on the stove, wondering if you fed the cat already, or is trying to write the screenplay for next year's Oscar winner, count your breaths. Try counting to the largest number you can imagine and if you lose count before you get there because the mind got distracted, start at 1 again. Don't dwell on what that number is, just start counting. The requirement is that you keep count as you advance toward the big number.

Here are some tips on counting your breaths. You can count each inhalation and each exhalation, only the exhalations or only the inhalations. It doesn't matter which one you choose and you don't have to use the same one every time you meditate or within the same meditation session. Whichever method you choose, the requirement is that you concentrate on keeping count. That helps keep thoughts out of your head a little but it's not infallible. You lose count eventually, don't you, whether at 3, 5 or 35 and then you're back to the stove, the cat or the screenplay.

Counting your breath, how to start breathing at the beginning of a sitting and what patterns of breathing work best are discussed in detail later because, together with physical immobility, breathing plays a major role in meditation under my method. But for now, let's leave it and stay with figuring out a physical posture that sends minimal stimulus to the brain.

So, back to posture: the horizontal posture, although not the most effective, has many advantages. Although it's a good one to fall back on when you just want to relax, it's been known to work for meditation for some people in certain circumstances. People with some physical impairment and old people may find this the most suitable alternative due to their various conditions. For folks with such challenges, it may help when lying even on carpeted floor if a firm mat, one to two inches thick, can also be placed under the body for additional comfort because that position usually needs to be maintained for quite a while—as long as 40 minutes. Sick and invalid people therefore could meditate lying down and even in bed, and if that means they can end up in a calm, peaceful mental condition, wide awake preferably, but even asleep for that matter, there's some gain in that!

In spite of the possibility of falling asleep, many people manage to meditate successfully in that position and even lying in bed. It works particularly well if, after a good night's sleep, you are wide awake in your bed and decide to meditate right there and then, before you get up. As an example, I sometimes meditate twice a day. My first session is when I first wake up. Lying in bed, I position myself comfortably (as described earlier), keep as still as possible and start exercising (as I will describe later). I do that for about 15 minutes and can usually get a few precious moments of stillness of body and mind. I find it even more relaxing than the sleep I've just had because I am awake to enjoy those moments. And then I meditate sitting up later in the morning or in the day. It can work.

Another situation that is well served, with a very positive outcome, is when you are simply unable to fall asleep. Meditating in that position in bed can be a very productive and rewarding experience. Talk about turning insomnia into gold!

But apart from these specific circumstances the horizontal position may still be sending too many signals to the brain for most people, especially beginners in good health, to be truly the most effective way to keep the body absolutely still. There are just too many parts of the body (back of the head, upper back, lower back, arms, the soles of your feet) that are in contact with something other than air, generating stimulus from those parts as you stay in that position for a prolonged period and stimulus is what we're trying to reduce to help the body stay still—very critical in meditation. So if you can, sit up when you meditate. Make lying down the exception rather than the rule.

Next, let's check out a part of the body that, although still sensitive, is quite used to bearing the body's weight and being in contact with something. Your feet are what you stand on, sometimes for long periods, so they are the next obvious choice. Let's stand up then and keep the body still. Stability becomes a problem with that choice unless you're one of Her Majesty's Coldstream Guards and if you try to solve that problem by using a wall, we're back to the first problem with stimulus from your back, back of the head, shoulder or forehead.

A Bum Deal

Which brings us to another area of your body used to bearing weight—your bum. Sit on it and you'll see it's one of the better options. Now what you need to do is to sit on it in a posture that is as symmetrical as possible. That's not because it looks good but because it produces optimal balance and stability. That way, your body has a decent shot at staying still for a prolonged period.

Here are several ways of sitting that can work, some better than others. Which one is the best one for you depends mostly on your physical makeup:

1. sit on a well padded chair or flat surface such as a relatively hard bed. Sit with your back straight. Don't lean on the backrest if there is one. Keep your legs apart at a comfortable angle for stability and your feet flat on the floor;
2. sit on one of those ergonomic kneeling posture chairs that young, hip computer hackers love;
3. sit cross-legged on a thick mat, with or without a smaller cushion right under your bum. Raising your bum above your knees makes it more comfortable although Indian Yogis seem to manage fine;

4. sit in the lotus position where the right foot rests on the left thigh and the left foot rests on the right thigh. Yeah, right—good luck.
5. sit in a half-lotus position where only one of your feet is resting on the opposite thigh;
6. sit with shin and feet resting flat on the floor, feet pointed toward each other.

If you need a visual of the lotus or half lotus or of an ergonomic kneeling posture chair, please Google it.

For all positions, keep the back straight. When sitting on the floor, with or without cushion, keep the legs and knees flat on the floor as much as possible. Lowering your shoulders and pushing your lower abdomen out help center the upper body. Always wear loose clothes because you don't want to restrict any part of the body or cause poor circulation. Wearing no pants helps folded legs be comfortable simply by having nothing in the folds. For men, get your balls strategically out of the way; crushing them sends very loud signals to the brain.

For Christians who are used to kneeling while they pray, that position may well be the best for meditation, whether using a prie-dieu, the pew at the local church or kneeling on some padding and resting your hands at chest level on a chair or stool. That is the original missionary position. Muslims may find prostrating themselves works best because that's what they're used to. Neither of these two positions is bad but they are not as good as sitting on your bum because for most people they are prone to deliver more stimulus to the brain from many parts of the body than sitting does. But if any of these is what works for you, it'll do just fine for meditating.

For optimal stability in sitting, take care not to lean in any particular direction. So, plant your body in the center as best you can. For comfort, sit up straight or follow the natural curve of your spine; to find that curve simply go by what feels the most comfortable to you. Ramrod straight is probably not the best option as it requires constant contraction of some muscles and the aim is to stay still in a relaxed posture, even though you'll be contracting certain specific muscles in the prescribed exercises. Comfort is bound to be different for each individual and is also often based on personal physiques and preferences, so experiment with various postures until you find the sweet spot that works best for you. And if any part of the body starts to hurt, it's probably because you are not sitting straight and your body is not centered, so make adjustments as much as you need to relieve the pain. It may require several sessions initially over a period of time to get rid of all discomfort and find the posture or postures that suit you the best.

Try different mats, cushions, chairs, beds, sofas also— anything that you can sit on. The goal is to sit very still in comfort for an extended period with the least stimulus going from the various parts of your body to your brain. So do find a position that works best for you (which may very well be one that I haven't even covered) and go with it. In meditation, you'll need to sit very still for as long as you can manage—up to 40 minutes per sitting—that's why finding how best you can sit in comfort is so important. It's also possible that a different position may feel better on different days depending on your physical and mental disposition at the time.

The size of the cushion you want to use is a very personal thing. A skinny person with just skin and bones as a blunt end is likely to require a thick one. A fat person with ample padding in that department may even be able to sit on a stone slab and be even more comfortable than your skinny friend.

After you've found a comfortable and stable way to sit, it's time to talk about how to become still.

In body first.

Then in mind.

Get Physical

The exercises recommended here apply regardless of which posture you adopt for your training in meditation, including lying down on the floor or in bed when you practice.

Now, to sit without moving at all for a long time is not possible because you still need to breathe. So let's address the question of how to breathe with as little body movement as possible. You will find that, generally, there are really only two major ways to breathe. You can use the chest muscles where you're flexing your rib cage or the abdominal muscles, by flexing your diaphragm. And of these two groups of muscles, using the abdominal muscles seems to result in lesser overall movement for most people.

Using the chest muscles causes the chest, and to a lesser degree, the shoulders, to rise when you inhale and to fall when you exhale. Using the abdominal muscles causes the belly to go out when you inhale and to retract when you exhale. From my own experience, I would recommend you use the abdominal muscles because in addition to causing less movement, you can get a lot more air into your lungs, which is always useful when exercising, and physical exercise is what you'll be doing. The bottom line is you need to breathe and you want to do it by moving your body as little as possible. By the way, if you choose to lay down when meditating you'll find that chest breathing can be just as good a choice simply because the forces of gravity work equally favorably for both chest and abdominal breathing when the body is in a horizontal position. But still, my vote goes to abdominal.

In due course, you may find that you're intermittently switching between the two sets of breathing muscles, favoring one set over the other as dictated by the body's disposition. So, if you're using your abdominals and find yourself switching to your chest muscles on and off, that's ok, don't fret over it. Go with the body, not the mind, and just switch back to using your abdominals if and when it feels right. You will eventually slow down your breathing as much as possible as a way of keeping the body dead still so in the end it may not matter much with method of breathing you choose. To start with however, in the initial stages of sitting when you're breathing normally, the abdominal muscles seem to cause less body movement.

To facilitate the flow of air through the nose into the lungs, it is best to pull the tongue back slightly—so that the tip of your tongue is touching the back of your upper front teeth. This will ensure that inhalation is unobstructed, but you may well be able to achieve the same thing just by relaxing the oral cavity. It seems it's even more critical to make sure the flow of air is unobstructed if you're lying down while meditating because in that position saliva and other nasal drainage can accumulate at the back of the throat. Do take care not to choke because that's called dying.

Now Work Those Muscles

So far, we've mostly covered keeping the body still as a means of keeping the mind still (as in not thinking) even in dealing with the act of breathing. Now let's address breathing in its own right and discuss the critical role it plays in the physical exercise involved in meditating. Here's the kicker: breathing IS the exercise, at least the way I want you to breathe when you meditate using my method. At a very high level, what you'll be doing is to:

1. count your breath;
2. slow down your breathing, and;
3. hold your breath.

By getting you to breathe that way I'm actually getting you to exercise—yes, to perform physical exercises, because the only way you can slow down your breathing or hold your breath is to use those breathing muscles (your abdominal muscles if you follow my recommendation). Later on, I describe various ways of controlling and modulating your breathing, and those too are just different ways of using or exercising those muscles.

Exercising one's muscles or physical exercise is known to be a relatively easy and predictable way to keep the mind focused and relatively still. Runners know this from experience; so do people who work out at the gym, windsurf or kite sail all day, scale rocks, ski slopes for hours, even if they have not tried to understand it intellectually or scientifically. Now, I know it may sound a little strange at first to hear me talk about breathing as a physical exercise but that is exactly what it is.

But as a form of exercise, it has a distinct advantage which makes it ideal for meditation. Using the various muscle groups that are required to ski, pump iron, perform gymnastics, windsurf or play basketball requires a relatively high level of mental activity with constant input, reaction, assessment, adjustment, response, etc. between the mind and the muscles. Additionally, those activities are often accompanied by an agenda called winning, the pursuit of which usually leads to mood swings ranging from joy, despair, anger to downright meanness. By comparison, using the abdominal muscles in the physical exercise called breathing actually requires very little or practically no input from the brain. Which is just as well or you would stop breathing when you're asleep.

The breathing muscles, therefore, are extremely independent of the brain. That makes them the best choice for the reciprocal control that is intermittently passed back and forth between the brain and the muscles. The brain is needed to concentrate the mind on exercising those muscles (breathing in certain specific ways) and the muscles are needed to focus the mind on a single activity to calm it down. That's what we are trying to achieve in meditation and the fact that exercising them entails the least amount of effort on the part of the brain to control them in the first place gives the mind the best shot at becoming quiet while engaged in that activity, gradually leading to lesser and lesser mental activity, and eventually to no activity at all—while you remain wide awake and continue to work out.

The use of those muscles to control your breathing basically means that you are performing a focused, and some may even say mindless physical exercise similar to running—in a positive sense. You are exercising or flexing your breathing muscles. Different exercises have varying degrees of "mindlessness". As examples, running requires more mental work than sitting, cycling probably more than running due to the greater speed if nothing else, and swimming probably more than cycling due to people not being able to breathe under water, drowning, sharks, etc. Correct or not, the point I'm making here is that sitting and breathing requires very little mental work, if you do it right. But if you don't do it right, you will find that breathing effectively from a meditation standpoint requires much more mental effort than most physical exercises you've ever done, to the point of being a virtually impossible task. So, take these instructions in very carefully and study them for ever while you develop your own routines.

One thing about physical exercise—e.g. sporting activities—is that when you participate in any of them, you always tend to feel better and relaxed afterwards (especially noticeable if the exercise followed a particularly rough day at the office!) I'm sure you've also done it on occasions just to "clear your head". The fundamental premise of my approach in meditation is based on that principle and essentially, we're using physical exercise when meditating to "clear the head".

Meditation does it particularly well—in fact, better than most other forms of exercise.

I cannot resist mentioning one particular exercise because it is closer to meditation than most and it is also one of my all-time favorites. Like meditation, it is performed slowly and it involves flexing your breathing muscles in controlling your breath and occasionally holding it for long periods of time. I always feel relaxed and quietly at peace after a snorkeling session. Fresh water, or that cold beer, tastes infinitely better after a few hours of exploring coral reefs and visiting with the fishes for more reasons than the obvious ones.

Now, we've all heard of this thing called runner's high, which can occur after the mind has been focused for a long time on very little other than the act of running. What we get in meditation is what I call *sitter's high*—yes, as you sit there, pumping those abdominal muscles over a prolonged period.

So, here's a synopsis of the principle: Neither the mind nor the muscles can do it alone. They take turns leading and following. The body, besides being kept still, is directed by the mind to work out in a very specific way—exercising the abdominal muscles in the act of controlled breathing. Working out with the abdominals constantly, the body sends repeating, monotonous signals to the brain and gets the mind to focus on a single external activity. Concentrating on the work out, the mind gradually drops almost all externally-caused internal stimuli altogether and then in due course creates no internally-caused internal stimuli of its own either. It focuses on working out and nothing else until it eventually focuses on nothing altogether. It can do that because, as mentioned earlier, breathing is an activity that requires no conscious direction from the brain. The motionless body, in due course, also ends up sending practically no stimulus whatsoever to the brain—especially at the point when you're holding your breath. At that exact moment, not only are you actually working out (i.e. flexing those abdominal muscles), but your entire body, your entire being in fact, is absolutely m-o-t-i-o-n-l-e-s-s. Putting your body and mind in that condition over and over again is what makes it possible for the mind to become totally blank, when it's entertaining no thought whatsoever, when it is totally still—even as you remain fully awake.

Ready, Set, Breathe

So let's get right into exercising your abdominal muscles. You start by counting your breathing as you keep your body still. I've already gone over counting just your exhalations, both exhalation and inhalation or just your inhalations but now I'm going to give you more specific instructions on breathing as your physical exercise as I describe what you actually need to do during meditation.

This is how I suggest you start your meditation session. Just as an athlete hyperventilates before performing his physical routine, whether it's gymnastics or a swimming race, I want you to do likewise or something similar:

1. use either set of breathing muscles (abdominal or chest) as you prefer for comfort or habit as it doesn't really matter at this point. Chances are you will intermittently switch back and forth between the two;

2. count your breath, again using any of the counting methods described;

3. exhale through the mouth, even noisily, if that's what feels right to you (generally, while meditating, your mouth is closed and you inhale and exhale through your nose);

4. keep hyperventilating while you count toward the big number;

5. after you've hyperventilated a few times (as many as you want) rather quickly, then when you're ready, take deep breaths. Start inhaling as deeply as you can, and when you exhale, try

to push all the air out of your lungs. Do that a few times also, not just once;

6. what I'm doing here is I'm getting you to fill your lungs with fresh air (oxygen) as many times as you feel necessary or just comfortable with in preparation for the physical exercise you will be doing next that will result in the normal oxygen deficiency arising from any form of exercise;

7. stop hyperventilating whenever it feels like you've done it enough—again like that athlete preparing for his performance—and just switch to normal breathing;

8. at this point, I suggest you go to abdominal breathing because, as explained earlier, of the two breathing methods, it's the one that involves lesser body movement overall and supplies more air to the lungs;

9. during this initial stage you should also take the opportunity to do all the scratching, twitching, coughing, clearing of your throat and nose, swallowing, stretching, bending, leaning this way, leaning that way, cracking your neck, fine-tuning your posture—all of the adjustments that you feel are necessary for settling into a comfortable, centered posture in preparation for the meditation physical workout. Now is also a good time to burp and fart. And of course, you're doing all of this fine-tuning as needed while you're hyperventilating and counting up to the big number.

How long should you hyperventilate? That's entirely up to you. For some people, it could be for a count of as low as 5 to 10, for most people probably closer to 20, and if you need to go even higher, have at it. It'll also probably vary from session to session. The thing is, it's not important, so you do whatever is comfortable or feels right for you. Do it until you naturally start to slow down your breathing. Then you can get into the other breathing patterns that are described below.

Even as you are breathing more slowly and counting toward the big number, chances are that thoughts will take over again, and you lose count. When that happens, as I said before, you just have to start at 1 again. When you start again, you can skip the hyperventilation part; that was only to start you off in the exercise. However, there is nothing wrong with hyperventilating more than once at the beginning of a session; it's an excellent way to over-supply your lungs with oxygen in preparation for pumping those abdominals.

Now remember this very important point which is one of the fundamental principles of this method of meditation: even though we talk about breathing and counting of breaths, in meditation terms, you are actually exercising those breathing muscles—again, preferably your abdominal muscles rather than your chest muscles.

Sitting Pretty

So now you're sitting pretty and you're exercising those abdominal muscles. While you're undergoing these cycles of losing count and starting all over again, whether you want it or not, calm will start to sneak into your general disposition—your physical disposition at first, and then later, your mental disposition.

Here's the overall pattern that will develop quite involuntarily when you're sitting. In repeating these counting cycles, each time your count reaches 5, 10 or higher, your breathing will gradually and automatically slow down again. You inhale and exhale more slowly and then you hold your breath on and off, and from this, a great variety of breathing patterns—i.e. of ways you are flexing those breathing muscles—will follow. Here are some breathing patterns that work well but expect many more to come out of your own instincts when you're doing it yourself:

1. Your exhalation is long and slow. At the end of your exhalation, you take a deep breath and start another long, slow exhalation;

2. Your exhalation is interrupted intermittently when you are holding your breath altogether for a while. At the end of such an exhalation, you take several breaths to make up for a temporary oxygen deficiency;

3. One long drawn-out exhalation is followed by a long drawn-out inhalation.

4. You breathe normally a few times and then at the point where you would normally inhale again, stop and hold your breath instead. After holding it for a while, instead of inhaling, continue to exhale and push all the air out of your lungs as much as you can, and then hold your breath again. Hold it for as long as you can, comfortably. Inevitably, you will have to take a few deep breaths quickly after that, but after you've recovered, try the whole routine all over again a few more times. You will find that with each repetition of this routine the stillness and calm you experience when you're holding your breath will get noticeably deeper.

If these patterns and others automatically develop for you, that's good, because the idea is to slow down your breathing and use different patterns when you meditate. That is what is needed in meditation. You can just let it happen or aim for it, wherever your mood or physical disposition takes you on the occasion. I describe a few others further below but I want you to really understand that although I've described those patterns above, the patterns that will work for you will come to you quite naturally—just use what I've described above as a general guideline of what to expect.

By the way, if you find that your breathing slows down sooner than is described above, or that you find it unnecessary to hyperventilate for your breathing to get into the desired patterns, then follow your instincts. But if you find yourself struggling with getting a slow breathing pattern going and starting to feel calm, then I suggest you give my recommended approach a shot. Still, the overall concept is that sooner or later you will inevitably develop your own breathing patterns that produce the same results. When you understand that you need to exercise those abdominal muscles and that using different breathing patterns is what does the job, your instincts will likely prevail and guide you along without requiring much input from the mind—the perfect scenario. And by the way, the discoveries you make of the methods, styles and nuances that work well for you could be part of Chapter Two.

These various exercises result in a state in which the body and the mind appear to be two separate entities passing control back and forth between them. Through the exercising of the breathing muscles, the body will capture the mind and hold it focused for a while but the mind will escape time and again and the chase will start all over again and all that is an integral aspect of this meditation technique. And by the way, when it comes to holding your breath, push yourself but stay reasonable. Don't compete with nature because you will lose.

And as you're now breathing very slowly, it takes a long time to get to 10. It would take forever to get to the big number. But taking forever to get to anywhere will start to not matter as you stop counting altogether and just breathe—more on this in a minute.

Time and again, you will lose count and the mind will wander back to the cat, your car, your work, the movie you saw last week. And that's ok. When you realize that your mind has taken you for a ride, once again make a fresh start, go from 1 and work up to those higher numbers. I've said this so many times because I want you to understand that this will happen over and over again, especially in the early stages of your training in meditation, so get used to it. Whatever you do, try to avoid getting agitated at this apparent failure; that would just make it harder to get to the stillness and calm that will emerge—that's a promise! So relax, focus on your workout and start at the beginning again.

The long exhalations are so critical that they deserve redundant coverage. Whether you choose to let a little bit of air escape from time to time and instinctively just hold your breath or to take one long continuous exhalation until you basically cannot push any more air out and then hold your breath at that point, or any of the other patterns, executing them again and again is the workout I want you to perform with those abdominals. The interruptions that are necessary for you to catch your breath because you need to make up for that temporary oxygen deficiency should not matter if once you've caught your breath you go straight into another repetition. Slowing, holding, controlling your breath amounts to exercising your abdominal muscles—it is the exercise I want you to perform. Yes, I know I'm repeating myself but the connection between those various breathing patterns and the physical exercise is the second part of the foundation of my method of meditation (the first part being keeping the body still).

Later, you'll discover that in meditation whether you're tensing those muscles only slightly or very hard will eventually not matter. Incidentally, every time I've spoken about holding your breath it's been after you've exhaled some air first. One breath manipulation feature that is specific to meditating horizontally is that holding your breath at the top, with your lungs full, can be done in comfort. You would probably have stumbled upon it yourself in your practice and experimentation sooner or later, but here it is. And there will be others that you will discover that I haven't mentioned or may never even come across myself. That's the nature of this journey called meditation.

Take A Ride

Eventually, generally after a degree of calm has sneaked into your sitting, counting your breaths will be replaced by something which in a way is more tangible and physically visible. You find yourself visualizing you lower abdomen slowly going in and out. And if you're still counting at that stage but counting the movement of the abdomen, you will find that even counting those will eventually fade away. That too may happen involuntarily but you can aim for it also or give in to it because it's quite the normal pattern and a pattern to follow with good reason. We've now come to the beginning of the next phase in exercising your breathing muscles.

Whether or not you're counting when you do this, visualizing your breathing can involve anything from actually watching your lower abdominal muscles heave to a more abstract vision of your midsection contracting and relaxing, to just being aware that you are breathing and exercising your breathing muscles in your mind's eye.

Now, there is a term I use for watching, focusing on, following, manipulating, modulating, controlling, and even playing with your breathing (i.e. using various ways to exercise those abdominal muscles) which is what you end up doing in visualizing your breathing. I call it *riding your breath*. From now on, that's what I mean whenever I use this term.

When you're riding your breath, you normally end up varying the way in which you're breathing even more imaginatively. You could be interrupting a long exhalation by occasionally tensing the lower abdomen a little more, using staggered inhalations which also tenses those muscles every time you interrupt the inhalation, or letting out in quick succession a series of exhalations. In other words, what you end up doing instinctively is playing with a multitude of ways of holding your breath to find alternative ways to work those breathing muscles.

So now you're riding your breath, you're flexing those abs, and you're concentrating on that job—yes, instead of "thinking" ordinary everyday thoughts that clutter the mind practically every waking hour you spend on earth. You're captivating your mind with your exercise instead of using it to think about the cat, your car, your credit card or investments, even that screenplay.

Catch Your Breath

Eventually, the counting will be no more. You are just "catching" your breath and riding it. I say catch in quotes because I don't mean it in the traditional sense where you're panting. I mean you've locked your mind's focus on it, and strange as it may sound, you start to "ride" it from the top of your breath to the very bottom of it, when you then literally catch your breath (now panting) to make up for the oxygen deficiency brought about by that long ride.

Here is a useful tip: in the middle of riding your breath quite happily, if the mind slips away to Hawaii and a spectacular sunset, tensing those lower abdominal muscles even harder than usual at that point can reel it back in and bring focus back to the ride. It works also with a mind that has wandered back to the office by dispelling narrative thoughts, memories and ideas that have suddenly reappeared from earlier musings. Constantly tensed up abdominal muscles breathing, in both inhalation and exhalation, is another breathing pattern that is really efficient in producing a calming effect because it engages the brain directly, immediately and quite forcefully. Now, here's an odd thing. Ruminating, contemplating and meditating have similar meanings if you check a dictionary. The cow appears to be contemplating when it performs the 'other' form of rumination. When you want to tense those muscles as suggested here, if you imitate our friend the cow with a bellow by saying or silently mouthing "Moooooo" you will find that it is one of the best ways to tense those muscles. Isn't that a funny coincidence? Or is it? All I can say is if you're one of those who believes there's really someone up there (or down there), I hope you see how she let her sense of humor get the better of her at least once during those six days. She must have spent a good part of the seventh day laughing about it.

I've mentioned it briefly before, but here's a corollary worth repeating that underscores why one specific aspect of the breathing patterns described works really well in meditation, which as you've already been told, also relies heavily on keeping the body still. When you hold your breath, you stop the movement of even the breathing muscles. At that point, there is total immobility. And that is a double bonus in meditation terms because at that particular point, your body is completely still AND you're tensing those breathing muscles. Nothing (external, at least) is moving! Frequent spells of this absolute immobility helps bring about certain physical and mental phenomena that are very important to successful meditation, which are described next.

Go Mental

The first phenomenon occurring in meditation that I want to bring up has to do with your hands. Your hands being kept still for a prolonged period, whether together or by your sides fully relaxed, as suggested earlier when we discussed posture, leads to an important condition in meditation. Your hands are very active agents of the brain in that they are used to make contact with everything as the means to introducing things, and sometimes people, to you. You tend to touch things with your hands when you first encounter them. If you're going to look at something more closely, taste it, smell it, listen to it, it's often your hands that act as the middleman. Some people even insist they need to use their hands to show their affection—at least that's their story and they're sticking to it. Holding them very still, resting on your lap or by your sides has a purpose. You're making sure that these normally active agents get deactivated. This treatment of them in meditation results in their feeling sort of heavy after a while. I call it the 'heavy-handed' stage. That is a good development. It is a good indication that you're getting somewhere and making good progress in your meditation because it usually precedes another condition which is a significant milestone in meditation. I've found that it usually means that the state of near-zero stimulus from your entire body is on its way and may be just around the corner.

Which brings me to the second phenomenon that is the milestone. It is connected with your entire body and results from having kept it dead still for a prolonged period. As the ride of your breath gets longer and longer, it will feel like you are exercising those lower abdominal muscles really hard when in reality you are not. At near-zero stimulus, the body feels like it weighs a ton or is made of a block of wood. Because it hasn't sent much stimulus to the brain for quite a while, the lightest of signals from it feels highly magnified at control central.

In due course, at zero stimulus from the body to the brain, you feel the presence of neither your hands nor your body. What follows is a state that starts to occur after you've meditated for a while when you suddenly realize that you don't feel your body any more, or rather, you become aware of the absence of the sensations usually coming from it. It's not numb, because you are also very aware of the fact that you can move any part of it whenever you want and no doubt you will test it and confirm it to be so. This is what happens when the various parts of the body have not been sending stimulus to the brain for a long time.

Drawing A Blank

When you get to this stage of zero-stimulus from anywhere, external or internal, to the brain, your breathing is almost imperceptible, your body would have been still for a long time. You will still be tensing those abdominals from time to time when you're holding your breath altogether. A pervasive calm should reign all over you at that point. You may come to a realization that you're not doing much at all, including thinking, and just as immediately drop even that thought. You may appreciate having a mind that is blank, that is aware but is not active, or simply feel at peace just being in that state. It's like your brain is sitting down and taking a break when it normally has to remain standing all the time. And you find that you can take thinking or leave it, at will. It's a very empowering sensation. It's the ultimate state of relaxation. How do you enjoy such control over your mind? Because of the very nature of this condition, you do and you don't.

And why is that? There is no why. There is nothing to figure out. There is no figuring out. To be or not to be? There is no question.

You've now reached your goal, the destination you set out for, the whole objective of your meditation. It's a bit of a paradox; your mind is blank because you want it to be blank—that is an impossible feat under 'normal' circumstances. You are also completely aware of yourself, of the fact that you are where you are, that you're part of something real. If you choose to go back to riding your breath, you can most willfully. A noise outside will be heard very distinctly but can lead to no other consequence in the mind because you will it so. Usually, life makes sense only when we are aware of who we are, what we are, where we are, in what timeframe we exist in relation to other people, a specific place and a multitude of events both near us and far away from us. In the depth of your meditation, you will have that same awareness, in much sharper focus, but it will not be in relation to anything or anybody because it doesn't have to be for life to make sense. When you experience this, it will make sense to you even though I'm not making any sense with what I've just described.

The Trip Home

As a beginner you may reach this level after you've been practicing meditation for a while—6 months or even longer, and even then get to this condition only after 20, 30 or 40 minutes into a session. Of course, this depends on the individual completely but I would say that I've given you the worst case scenario here. Chances are you will experience this earlier, as long as you practice regularly and diligently—and that means at least once a day.

These phenomena can take a slightly different form if you are lying down versus sitting when meditating. When lying down, more of your body is in contact with something (the floor or the bed) and if in bed, you may also have a sheet or blanket over you. All these points of contact may manifest themselves before the total absence of stimulus sets in. The feel of the sheet on your knees, the weight of the blanket on your chest, the feel of your soles on the floor or carpet, your back, the back of your head, your elbows, your hands in contact with the floor, all may send different signals than when you're sitting on your bum, before signing off as it were. Be aware of the different possibilities and take them as they come. But eventually, all sensations will die away if you maintain stillness in your body and the brain is engaged solely with riding your breath, which progresses into just riding air based on what it feels like to me, brought about by your exercising of those abdominal muscles in absolute stillness.

The longer you practice meditation the less uncomfortable it becomes to sit still for prolonged periods of time. This means that you leave the stage of counting your breath and get to the advanced stages of riding it sooner and also more often. It also means that you get to stilling the mind sooner and more often too when you sit. Progress in your training means that you're riding air in five minutes, you get heavy-handed in ten and get to the zero stimulus stage when you can start to enjoy the benefits of a still mind in fifteen, versus getting there in forty. It's a lot easier to get a still mind and enjoy it when your bum is not sore.

By the way, I've been referring to a session as being in the 20 to 40 minute range based purely on my own experience and tolerance level, meaning that by minute 40, my bum is begging for its life and pleading for the feet to take over. I don't know this for sure but I suspect that if you are able to tolerate longer sittings when you are just starting your training in meditation, you would probably progress faster, provided it's not a case of your having to sit that long every time to get anywhere in your practice. And as stated earlier, the more advanced you get in your training, the shorter your sessions will be simply because you're in the zero-stimulus, still mind state within a shorter time.

The Secret Of My Failure

I don't know where the training ends; maybe it never ends. So even though you may appear to have reached a relatively advanced stage in meditation, other obstacles can surface. Every stage brings its own challenges, and it would seem you will have to devise your own way of overcoming them.

The best way I can think of to explain what I mean is to illustrate it with an example from my own experience. After I felt that I had left the beginner stage, I suddenly found that for a while the better I got, the worse things seemed to be. I had got quite good at staying very still and riding my breath and found myself being able to be in control of that state. So much in control in fact that I no longer had to struggle to stay focused on riding air and was able to start thinking again while remaining in that state. Start thinking again! Think about that! That is NOT what I want to do! And thus began another round of "back to basics" as I started from that point to try and bring the mind back to focus on my exercise, on counting my breaths, on the actual ride and eventually back on nothing again. So even though I was enjoying stillness of body and mind, I was not out of the woods!

When that happens to you, know that you're not alone and renew your effort. The match is between your body and brain versus mind and ego and the game promises to be a tough one. When you're in that state of zero or near-zero stimulus from the body, you're so relaxed that thinking becomes easy, even comfortable. That's when you need to maintain, or renew if necessary, your effort to concentrate on your ride as that's the only way you'll get to the next stages in meditation. This effort can take the shape of imitating the cow with a bellow or taking up counting to the big number again even as you are holding your breath. As I said earlier, use whatever you've developed yourself that you know to work.

So what are you experiencing? What are you likely to remember experiencing? Total calm. As mentioned in the list of mental states: You're standing at the bottom of the Grand Canyon, in Yosemite, among giant Sequoias, on a glacier, by a thundering waterfall, inside a cathedral—all by yourself, in absolute silence, yet not alone or lonely. And you can stay there for as long or as briefly as you want—a decision you have the luxury of making instinctively.

All the while, just sitting in a room.

At home.

This is how you meditate.

This is why you meditate.

Other Incidental Factors

Because the success of meditating is generally based on reducing stimulus to the brain, I suggest you reduce or eliminate the visual stimulus also by having your eyes closed when you're flexing those abdominals. It would probably be easier to visualize your breathing as well that way.

Again, for the sake of reducing or eliminating stimulus to the brain, protect the body from cold or heat when you're sitting by wearing clothes appropriate to the climate. Loose clothing that does not restrict movement or blood circulation, especially in your legs, is highly recommended. You don't have to wear a robe or a tunic or a monk's garb whether orange, black, white or purple in color—just something loose and comfortable, and suitable for the current conditions, and if that's a robe or a tunic, so be it—have no hang-up either way. There is just no need to go Hollywood.

If you have a cold or the sniffles, the nasal passage may be blocked, making it difficult to breathe easily or comfortably. In that case just sit for only as long as you're comfortable.

As for diet that may help or hamper meditation, I don't have much to say other than I don't see it being different from the general consensus or conventional wisdom regarding food, supplements, drugs, alcohol and dietary practices. I suspect eating grass like a cow is not going to help you meditate or ruminate better. Smoking grass may make you feel calm for a while but in the long run makes you dependent on ingesting a chemical from outside your system and if you get addicted, your supply is gone and your dealer is 5 miles offshore on his yacht . . . The only thing I can think of is since breathing is such an integral part of exercising those breathing muscles, a smoker's cough is not going to help. So whether it's alcohol, over-eating, starving yourself, eating junk food, health food, a vegetarian or a vegan diet, smoking pot, shooting the hard stuff, stay with the advice of your Mom and your doctor. Then just meditate.

Avoid intense sitting—i.e. sitting for longer than is comfortable for you. After all, this is about relaxing, stilling the body, stilling the mind. So if you cannot catch a decent ride after several attempts, go feed the cat or pay those bills and try again later.

If at first you find that you can only sit for less than 5 minutes, I suggest that is all you do. The trick is to go back and try again the next time. The next time can be an hour later, 12 hours later or the following day.

Although we've emphasized that stillness of body is a major factor in meditation, if it itches, scratch it. If any part of the body hurts, move and adjust your posture to alleviate it. If your mouth gets flooded with saliva, swallow. If your throat is itchy or ticklish, cough or clear it. You will find those acts do not interfere with the ride as long as you keep making an effort to focus on the ride as best you can.

Physical fitness must be a plus for meditation if only because you will breathe better or more easily, probably be able to hold your breath longer—extending those periods of absolute immobility that are so vital in meditation. Flexibility, nimbleness means you can probably sit more symmetrically and longer in greater comfort. However, it is no guarantee for successful meditation; training and practice is still necessary. So if you run, cycle, play basketball, volley ball, soccer, tennis or work out at the gym, that'll probably help you in meditation because that's just the way the body works and the way it gets the mind to follow. Even better are karate, Tai Chi or Chi Kung, not because of some mysterious Eastern connection between these forms of exercise and meditation but because they don't require much space, can be done in the privacy of your home or backyard and do not require special shoes, shiny bright clothing and coordination with other people's schedules. Yoga is different because it is more like meditation itself, but for me, it has the disadvantage of the physical demands it makes on the body—most of the postures it requires you to put your body in are more strenuous than sitting on your bum. Still, many people practice it, love it and reap benefits that are similar to what is derived from the meditation technique recommended in this primer. Go with whatever works for you.

When you're good for a 20- to 40-minute sit, shoot for doing it on a regular basis and try not to go longer than a day between sittings if you can. Just as in running, swimming, cycling, karate and other forms of physical exercise, the key to becoming good at sitting is to do it often and to do it regularly. So try to sit every day because that's how you get used to sitting still for a relatively long time. That way, you get good, comfortable sittings that allow you to exercise those lower abdominals for a prolonged period.

We've come to the end of the instructions on how to meditate, Before I indulge myself on sharing my views on meditation, which are entirely unnecessary in order for you to succeed in meditation, here's a short and quick recap of what to do and what happens when you meditate:

1. find a quiet place;
2. get into a comfortable posture;
3. sit very still;
4. count your breath;
5. slow down your breathing;
6. hold your breath (which amounts to tensing your abdominal muscles);
7. ride your breath;
8. you're working out with those abdominal muscles over and over again;
9. when you hold your breath, there is absolute immobility AND you're exercising;
10. your mind is totally focused in your physical exercise;
11. zero stimulus from body and mind occurs and stops all mental activity;
12. your mind is absolutely still and you're wide awake;
13. your mind gets a break and you are awake to enjoy it!

When you're working at this for 20, 30, 40 minutes and these calm physical and mental conditions finally prevail, you're meditating successfully. One last bit of instruction about these instructions: study them, remember them, use them to meditate successfully, use them to bring your mind back in line when it starts to wander but don't be thinking about them or going over them during meditation. Execute them—that's not the same as thinking about them while you're meditating.

The End Is Near

The two final sections cover some facets of meditation that I would like to go into a little before I end my thoughts on how it's done but I do so with some reservation because it deals with the *effect and consequences of practicing meditation* and I suspect that meditation affects different people differently and so I may be wasting your time like those extraneous chapters in those other books do. The only consolation I will take and excuse I will hide behind is that I would only be wasting your time for a few pages. So here goes.

That Empty Feeling

You may have noticed that the last mental state in Appendix A is 'Empty'. A quick explanation should probably be given to clarify its meaning here.

In meditation, feeling empty is not the same as having an empty feeling in the regular sense, nor does it mean the inability to feel anything. It means being able to wipe the mind clean of emotions derived from likes and dislikes, which are in turn based on preconceptions, discrimination and judgment. It means to clear the mind, to empty the mind. The effect of being able to empty the mind like this is two-fold:

1. It allows you to better appreciate the good feelings—i.e. you take in the experience fully with nothing blocking it—with no bias or preconceived notion or preference or hang-ups or comparisons;

2. It also makes it possible, or easier, to better bear or control the bad feelings—i.e. you fully experience the bad feeling, whether the result is sadness, emotional pain, anger, embarrassment, but you can let go and not dwell on it. You simply fill the place it occupies in your mind with calm, stillness, emptiness.

Yes, a good night's sleep would also do a decent job of that as your Mom would tell you and she would be right. Mastering meditation will let you do so at will, without skipping the realities of life or losing out on the human emotions that make us, fortunately and unfortunately, different from our cousins, the insects, birds, fish, animals and plants. In meditation, empty means an inactive mind, a mind at rest, at peace, even while you're fully awake and aware.

Running On Empty

In meditation, running on empty is the ultimate mental state to be in, the final destination all the time, the end of one journey and the beginning of a more exciting one, because now you've gone beyond *sitting* on empty, which is what you do when you're training, and are now *living and running* on empty. So what benefit is to be derived from a calm mind resulting from meditation? Before we go there, allow me a small diversion as a way of introducing how I think people benefit from the fruits of their meditation labor.

I would like to bring back a few things that I've previously touched upon here and there in this primer: the heavy hands, the body that weighs a ton, the sensation that zero stimulus from the entire body produces, the sense of calm in riding air from the top to the bottom of your breath, the enhanced sensitivity of the various parts of your body. This all has to do with how a clear, calm and blank mind senses things—not interprets or perceives, but senses things. You are sensing things like a child does, as opposed to perceiving them, which involves judging, comparing, assessing, measuring, discriminating things and people in accordance with a scale that you have created as you grew older and wiser and carry around in your head. And you are sensing the world around you in a very sharp, enhanced and, in a way, a magnified and yet focused mode—and all simply because of that state of mind brought about by meditation. I finally understood what Bob Dylan meant when he sang: "Ah but I was so much older then, I'm younger than that now."

When you're operating in that mode, sunlight on your skin can feel like you're being warmed by an invigorating source of energy, a rose can appear like it's displaying its splendor in the grass for your private viewing, music can sound like it was written just for you, words can have meanings that were previously hidden and are still hidden to the masses but have been revealed to you, and sometimes even voices from somewhere, usually from above, seem to be addressing you directly (I talk about this a little more later with a theory I have). All of these are the result of the condition of the mind as described in the previous paragraph. When that happens, do yourself, me and the world a favor. Don't go religious or all spiritual and wander around the place thinking you're in what they call a state of grace and attribute all this to some spiritual power, some doctrine, rite or ritual, some supernatural higher being or alien from another galaxy that controls the destiny of mankind, but for some reason, has chosen you as somebody who is special or for a special mission and feel you must at all costs hook up with Katie or Kelly. Just give credit where credit is due—to nature. Okay, I'll make one concession—your true nature. Because, my friend, that's all it is—nothing more, nothing less.

I have a story of my own regarding the supernatural that I want to share with you. Once, when I'd made good progress during a sitting, I suddenly felt a bright, warm glow slowly surrounding me completely, as if I was about to experience my own private version of the burning bush or some other celestial event. I opened my eyes very slowly as if to better receive such a gift from some mighty being from the other side and immediately realized that it was just the sun had come out. It was overcast when I started sitting. Watch out for the supernatural or the divine. This is just meditation—to stop that constant buzz in the head called unproductive thinking and nothing else. But there was a reason I "felt" what I felt. As described earlier, in or near the zero-stimulus state, the slightest signal from anywhere on the body gets highly magnified to the brain so the warmth on my skin, the light "seen" through my closed eyelids, the smell of the warm air, all felt like something special—and they were special. Naturally special. Plus, a calm, clear mind was able to receive them in all their glory like a child is able to do all the time but not us wise, older and sophisticated people. Remember it?

On a practical level however, when I say that's all it is, it is quite a lot; most likely a whole heap more than what we currently have for many of us, myself included, in the regular course of our existence in our individual circumstances. Imagine, in that enhanced state of mind and operating mode, potentially how much more productive you could be at your job, more attentive to your family and friends, to your enemies even. And if you're in public service or in the performing arts, imagine how much more genuine, inspiring and moving your 'performance' could be. Actors long for a condition they call being in the moment when they are performing. After meditating, there are times when you cannot help but be in the moment in everything you do. Now there are people who can get all this and be all this without meditating, and if you're one of those, then good for you. I envy you! But my point is *anyone* can get it with meditation—anyone, including you and me!

So, meanwhile back at the ranch, as a calmer (sounds like Karma but I do mean calmer) person, you're likely to get less stressed out, and more often than not, to take everything on a more even keel, whether at work, at home or in your personal relationships. I think that would be a good thing. But the idea is not you meditate, you get better and so now you're ok and you're done. You can always get better at meditation—to the point of stilling the mind in a single breath—and you can always improve as a person, so continue to practice. You will keep having a few of those bad days at the office and meeting those characters who just know that the world revolves around them and look at you questioningly with "which part of 'I'm the center of the universe' don't you understand"? How nice it would be to not be affected by such people and be able to treat them as if they are the center of the universe along with everybody else.

I have no concrete evidence that meditation is also good for your physical health. You decide if that is the case and your opinion is the one that matters. I personally believe that as a calmer person, you think clearer, are less prone to judge and so can be more compassionate toward your fellow man and fellow animal, you love better, fight better, and I believe, eventually, even die better.

Another corollary supporting the result of meditation on the mind: do you find sometimes that after a good night's sleep, things are clearer, good ideas pop up, solutions are found or suddenly you understand? That is the result of a clear head—that comes out of a calm, uncluttered mind. Meditation calms the mind, skipping the sleep part altogether. Imagine the possibilities!

Having advised you to steer clear of the supernatural and superstitions and all that gobbledygook, here is something that I do want to mention and put in perspective as best I can. If you ever find yourself having visions or thoughts that come out of nowhere but are somehow relevant to you or are enlightening, consider this possibility. This is my theory. I don't know if it's correct. Maybe some scientist can explain, confirm or disprove it some day but here's what I get from events that I have witnessed in my 60 years. Our brain, through evolution and procreation, is the recipient of thousands of years of human mental activity. That has to be true simply because we are here today. Mental activity is electrical activity. Can there be some residual activity of so long ago, in the distant past, that is very faint by now, so faint in fact that we no longer can detect it, let alone interpret any of it any more—stored in the deepest recesses of the brain, as it were? Well, my sense is that there is but we cannot detect it any more because the mind is constantly being assaulted by the kerfuffle associated with daily living, especially modern living. But reduce the buzz in the brain and the frenzy in the mind, who knows what can follow? Is it possible that in that state you can detect those residual, faint signals that are still actively transmitting that you would not "normally". With a calm mind or a blank mind even, brought about by meditation, what distant signals may you be able to detect? What can you hear or remember? You tell me.

Part two of the theory: electrical activity or brain waves are external and travel—I think. Is it possible for one person to "receive" another person's signals? Does that explain how Zen masters can tell when their students' brains are emitting Alpha, Beta or Theta waves in meditation? Beats me. I'm just looking for some peace and quiet on the way to the 'Big' peace and quiet.

So, if you do hear or remember anything, whatever that is, perhaps you could consider this theory as the possible cause of it instead of going the supernatural or paranormal route, or trying to contact ET. Do note also that if you do detect such faint signals, that's all they are and nothing more. Any information gleaned from them need not necessarily be more relevant, meaningful or have any special significance. Use that information with discretion and as you would anything you're hearing now from any source.

I am more than convinced that meditation has nothing to do with religion but I suspect it has everything to do with science, as in biology, chemistry, physics, electricity, electro-magnetism, etc. So I do have a question that is scientific in nature. Is there some chemical process involved in meditation? That is a question to which I don't have an answer because I am not particularly well read in the sciences. There's bound to be a ton of literature on the Web if you want to pursue it beyond my casual mention here. That the brain works in terms of electrical activity is known but is there also some chemical compound that is generated, induced, manufactured or enhanced depending on the various states that the brain is operating in? I find interesting that the brain can be induced to operate in certain ways though (and certain feelings created in humans) through the ingestion of externally produced chemicals (e.g. such drugs as opium, hash), so why not extend that idea to the possibility that these or similar chemicals are present, albeit not ingested but manufactured by the body naturally, when the same brain is induced to operate in the same manner through a natural process such as meditation?

Ok, these are not instructions, will not help you meditate so it's time to get off the soap box, but if you want to argue some more, there is always Appendix B. I wish you the best in your quest.

CHAPTER TWO

Your Journey

Appendix A

Mental States That Would Drive Sane and Insane People To Meditate

Here is a random list of some mental states that people may experience at various times in their lives (some of which it would be nice to get some relief from) as well as the better ones that are worth shooting for whether through meditation or other means:

FEELING	EXAMPLES OF CAUSES
Guilty	You remember how you cut your partner out of a deal twenty years ago. You are now a millionaire and he is homeless person.
Ashamed	You witnessed a thug abusing an old lady and robbing her of what little money she had and you turned away.
Embarrassed	In the absolute silence of the church, just before the bride's turn to say "I do", you fart.
Emotional	This is an assortment of feelings. You're trying to talk your child out of taking hard drugs and can't concentrate on just the biological damage they cause. Instead, you feel he's letting you down, shattering your dreams, ambitions, reputation and your heart aches from the sight of him as a shadow

	of his old self and what he could have been, what you've always hoped he would be.
Self-conscious	You're the last one to arrive at the meeting, the only vacant chair is miles away right next to the Chairman at the head of the conference table and as you crawl towards it you know people are analyzing your clothes, extra weight, hair, nose, the way you walk. You don't know what to do with your hands, where to cast your eyes and can't decide what's worse: throw up right here or see everyone stare at you even more as you run out and make for the men's room.
Self-pity	All your college buddies are now executives but you're stuck in lower middle management because you just chose the wrong company, the wrong field and your bosses just do not understand the huge contribution you've made all these years to the success of the company
Mean	You're about to interview a candidate who fired you for personal reasons at your last job
Spiteful	You're about to reject a loan application by your ex and her boyfriend
Angry	You've just been cheated out of your life savings

Uptight	Things are not going your way, you need validation badly, you think you deserve more than anyone else but nobody is paying any attention to you.
Obsessed	The new girl at the office is on your mind all the time. You can't work, eat, sleep, drive or go to the bathroom without thinking about her
Desperate	You're out of work and can't feed the family or pay the rent
Panic-stricken	You're picking your kid up from school and nobody can find her
Anxious	The rumor is your job has also been outsourced
Bewildered	Your stomach is on fire, you're at the emergency room but no one is paying any attention to you, nor do they seem interested or appreciate the seriousness of your condition.
Pained	Your lower back hurts so much you can't even lie down
Worried	People with the same qualification and experience as you have been interviewed for the past two weeks but there is no word from your boss.
Scared	The plane you're riding in is having engine troubles
Frightened	You're in your tent and you see a bear coming toward you
Harassed	The toilet is backed up, there is no hot water, the car won't start and you're late for an important meeting

Stressed	You've already put in 14 hours, the work is not finished, the bosses are waiting and the client has arrived
Agitated	You're in line for 15 minutes, only one teller is serving customers, there are five others chatting away behind her
Disappointed	Your colleague got the promotion you were longing for
Jealous	Your rival got the promotion you were hoping for
Exhausted	You haven't been able to fall asleep for three days in a row
Annoyed	Your neighbors are having a very loud party next door
Bored	You're not doing anything, have nothing to do, have nowhere to go, nobody to visit, nobody's visiting
Proud	You're buying the biggest house in your friends' neighborhood
Thrilled	You're racing down a slope skiing, flying solo in your plane for the first time, pulling off a jibe off a huge swell windsurfing
Moved	You're watching a great play, movie, TV show
Tickled	You're watching a performance by a comedian
Inspired	You're reading some religious scriptures
Stimulated	You're listening to a preacher
Captivated	You're listening to an inspiring politician

Amused	You just saw a funny commercial
Engrossed	You're reading a good book, playing your favorite game, performing a task you love, doing Tai Chi, Yoga, Chi Kung, working out, pumping iron, running, jogging, playing a sport
Fulfilled	Your daughter just graduated from college
Relieved	Your son finally graduated from college
Satisfied	You've just finished eating your favorite meal, with a glass of fine wine
Relaxed	You're listening to your favorite music, walking on the beach with your loved one, getting a massage, stroking your pet
Peaceful	You've just been to church, mosque, the temple
Calm	You're standing at the bottom of the Grand Canyon, among giant Sequoias, on a glacier, by a thundering waterfall, inside a cathedral—alone, all by yourself
Nothing	You're fast asleep, not dreaming, nor having a nightmare
Empty	You're wide awake and are meditating successfully

Appendix B

I Hurt, Therefore I Rant

What you read in this Appendix are purely my observations, thoughts and opinions and please treat them as such. Whereas I am quite serious about the instructions and pointers I compiled for your use to get you meditating successfully, the things I'm saying in this section are definitely not needed for that.

Many other forms of activity also bring calm to the mind besides the relatively strenuous ones connected with physical exercise and sports. Examples of regular, normal, everyday ones include knitting, reading a book, drawing, painting, solving a jigsaw puzzle, Sudoku, crossword puzzle, gardening, a walk in the park with your best friend—whether two- or four-legged. And they are all useful and good for the noggin.

And then there are other forms of activity that are somewhat more prescribed, manufactured, made up or invented. They include prayers, spinning a prayer wheel, mantras, quotes from books considered holy like the Koran, the Bible, the Torah. These were introduced by people in the tribes of old that claimed they had special insight into what some higher power wanted or demanded of people. Even though you can tell the view I hold of these practices from the way I just introduced them, the references I have made to them elsewhere in this primer and how I make light of them generally, I don't mean to say that they were unnecessary. There have been genuine proponents of those practices who were wise enough to realize that something needed to be designed for the masses who couldn't work it out for themselves, because they didn't have the time or the wherewithal, so they too can calm or soothe their minds. I'm not going to discuss the 'other' proponents who sold them to the masses in order to subdue them or for some other selfish agenda—you can find ample instances of such shenanigans yourself. Generally, I have no objection to the concept behind these inventions. But I am concerned about some of the consequences that have come out of their institutionalization. The formation of Corporate Christi, the distinction of sects even within the same faith, whether Muslim, Christian or Buddhist, the interpretation of old documents, as if their mere age renders them true, and the subsequent fallout from all the institutionalization of these inventions have led to wars, crusades, jihads, persecutions and ethnic cleansing, to David turning into Goliath, to two types of Irishman. History books as well as current newscasts sadly provide too many examples of the point I'm making.

But forgetting the sad consequences in the big picture, I sincerely believe that you can achieve the same or similar results through praying and those other practices that you can get out of meditation. Still, more often than not, they involve learning texts, rituals or elaborate ceremonies or worse still, having to belong to those same institutions, dress a certain way, serve time or make compulsory contributions, whereas you don't have to learn how to breathe, hold your breath or count.

The road to achieving a clear and calm mind under any of these alternatives, including meditation, may in the end be just as easy or as arduous. Meditation is just simpler in every respect and is definitely an individual undertaking where you are beholden to no one except yourself in its practice and does not sway you one way or the other in the fulfillment of your civic duties in society. Hopefully, this primer finds you free to choose as you please.

I remember reading an article in the National Geographic some years back on Jerusalem. Besides the natural attributes of the place, its people and the political conflict that exists there, it also covered and interviewed the visitors of all faiths who went there on a pilgrimage. It was reported that it was a very special place for many and that many of those interviewed responded they felt the presence of something or someone special for which they have no explanation, except to say that they believed they had a religious experience that cemented their faith. The reporter also interviewed a doctor at one of the clinics in the city and asked him what the difference was between what was characterized as a religious experience and mental illness or instability for which this doctor treated many people. His response was, "None". I think he was a secular Jew. I've never forgotten that story because for the first time in my life, through a piece in a magazine of some scientific repute, I got to hear someone express an opinion that confirmed what my instinct had gradually led me to conclude over the course of my years of observing animals, humans and society in operation. That this proclamation came, not from some hip youth attending UC San Jose or Santa Barbara, but from a man who practiced nitty-gritty medicine in a hospital was sobering, and out of Jerusalem, of all places! I wonder if there is a doctor in Mecca or in The Vatican City that this reporter could also interview.

That nudged me to include a suspicion of mine in this primer. A quick look at both historical and current trends shows a multitude of human preoccupations for which I suspect meditation could well be a viable alternative. Examples, both religious and secular, include the worshipping of Art, the female form, the male form, royalty, movie stars, pop stars, sons of gods, sons of heaven, gods, God, Vishnu, Krishna, Allah, moolah, the Father, the Son and the Holy Ghost, Saints Peter, Paul & Mary, old Lucifer, the Devil, Demons, bead fondling, appeasing or appealing to higher powers, chanting, praying, speaking in tongues, speaking to space aliens, getting a tarot card reading, sacrificing a goat, sacrificing a human, sacrificing oneself—this is just the beginning of the list.

And then there are those huge stone, steel, glass or crystal glittering structures erected to honor those invisible entities, for group prayers, chanting, singing with or without guitars or organs, for individuals of exalted status in flowing robes to read about extraordinary beings and events, jumping up and down, rolling around in a trance. And what about those arenas built for the pleasure of watching people fight to death or chase or hit a ball around in, watching a story or action being played out, people singing and playing music, people telling funny or unusual stories—the list goes on for ever.

They all have one thing in common: to engage, possess, control, ease, distract or soothe man's mind. If you have any doubt about what I just said, here's an example which is at the bottom of the totem pole in the mind repo business and yet confirms it succinctly. This is an ad for a movie in the LA Times on Thanksgiving Day, 2009 and it reads: "If you go to the movies to be INSPIRED and feel WONDERFUL, 'THE BLIND SIDE' will make you very happy." There is nothing wrong with it or what it's doing but I rest my case. See, meditating does the same thing, with a lot less baggage and in a simple, efficient way. Now, even if not all, but a good portion of those resources that have been used in those pursuits could be devoted to relieving real and not imaginary suffering—starving children, sick children, children orphaned by wars, people battered by the natural elements, societies that cannot grow enough food, economic models that can no longer provide dignity through work, just as a few examples—what would the world look like today? What do you think?

But, in the end, if you need to hang on to some personal symbolism to feel you belong, to ease your mind, to know that you are special because you are white, black, yellow or brown, a Catholic or Zen Buddhist, or a Boston Tea Partier or a member of the Fifth Street Gang, that you are one of the Chosen People or you belong to the Master Race, it pains me to think that I may not be able to reach you with this primer. It's rather sad, both for you and for humanity in general.

Clinging to such ideologies, especially when taken to the extreme, has often led to and continues to lead to much misery in life, inflicted upon yourself as well as on others who do not happen to cling to the same things as you. History, both ancient and current, and the news that's broadcast every single day from around the world, prove that over and over again. But even if you are of that disposition or inclination, do you think you can give meditation a shot anyway? What have you got to lose? If you can be a runner and still cling to any of the above, you can also be a sitter and do likewise, no?

The meditation training recommended in this primer belongs to the group of activities listed at the beginning of this section. It has no religious significance whatsoever even if it looks like it is based on meditation practices that have traditionally been associated with Eastern religions. You can hold any religious beliefs or none and still meditate successfully. It is simply a way of calming the mind in our everyday lives as we rush around chasing that paycheck in the rat business that inevitably turns into a race in which we're trying to get in front of our own shadow with the sun behind us. There may be scientific, biological or chemical similarities between meditating and several religious practices but that would be all—nothing else. There are no sacred cows (just regular cows), saints, demons, the devil, the undead, werewolves, vampires, virgin prizes, virgin births, divine legacy, promised land, resurrections, 400 year-old individuals, sins, absolutions, penance, second comings, first comings for that matter, Word (not the text processor but as in, first, there was . . .) sun gods, moon gods, holy scriptures, holy cardinal point, holy day, holy time, divination, pre-ordination, astrological lineups, destiny, karma, heavenly creatures or heavenly signs to embrace or denounce in meditation. Just nature, human cells, sinews, organs—blood and guts, as it were—brain cluttered by mind, mind blinded by ego, ego nurtured by man's ability to reflect. There may be a scientific cardinal point due to Earth's electro-magnetic field but that's another book altogether.

But if meditation must be thought of as some form of religion by any reader who simply cannot let go, then at least consider it non-denominational. You can therefore meditate in a Catholic church, a Protestant church, a Synagogue, a Mosque, a Hindu temple, a Buddhist temple, a Jehovah's Witness hall and any other Fellowship or Congregation hall as long as they don't throw you out for sitting around apparently doing nothing useful and not putting anything in the collection box. But then, what's wrong with a quiet room at home?

I've come to liken meditating to climbing to the top of a mountain (indulging in some mumbo jumbo to make a point) where we are told you can get a clear view of life and death. Then after having studied, trained and practiced for a fair while and having only managed to scale the foot of this mountain, I was nonetheless pleasantly surprised that even at the top of the foot, the view was quite telling. Since then, I'd like to think that I reached halfway up on several occasions, and at those moments, I caught a glimpse of a view that made me want to make the climb again and again—not necessarily to reach higher but just to climb again. A part of me suspects it would be nice to get to the top, but at the same time, the climb itself is such a thrill and is so refreshing that another part of me is already quite happy with what I already got. Unlike the runner who starts to get good and wants to see if he can run a marathon, I'm more like a runner who just loves to run because every foot, yard and mile is just there to be enjoyed. All I can say is the views I've had already are enough to keep me high above many of my daily trials and tribulations and that's more than I had before I stumbled upon the method proposed in this primer. So remember that even though the view from the top of the mountain is said to be breathtaking (again, no pun intended) I think you will also like the views from the various altitudes that you will attain while you practice your climbs. So start practicing as soon as you finish reading this primer and enjoy. Well, maybe one day I will reach the top and see that view. Hey, maybe we'll run into each other up there!

Made in the USA
Charleston, SC
12 January 2010